*This book is dedicated to the men and women who serve
and sacrifice every day to keep America free.*

Executive Producer
Charles James Schaefer IV

Associate Producers
Merrill Hughes Smith
Rich Galen

Picture Editor
Lynden Steele

Produced by Epicenter Media,
an imprint of Epicenter Communications.
www.epicenter.com

Visit Tyndale's exciting Web site at www.tyndale.com

TYNDALE is a registered trademark of Tyndale House Publishers, Inc.

Tyndale's quill logo is a trademark of Tyndale House Publishers, Inc.

George W. Bush: Portrait of a Leader

George W. Bush: Retrato de un líder

ISBN-10: 1-4143-0983-X (hc) English language edition

ISBN-13: 978-1-4143-0983-5 (hc) English language edition

ISBN-10: 1-4143-1015-3 (hc) Spanish language edition

ISBN-13: 978-1-4143-1015-2 (hc) Spanish language edition

Printed in the United States of America

11 10 09 08 07 06 05

7 6 5 4 3 2 1

George W. Bush

Portrait of a Leader

The First Four Years of the Presidency
As Seen by the White House Photographers

Foreword by Karen Hughes

Tyndale House Publishers, Inc. Wheaton, Illinois

President George W. Bush surveys the damage to the Pentagon following the 9/11 terrorist attacks from aboard the presidential helicopter, Marine One.
September 14, 2001

Foreword

By Karen Hughes

Pᴙᴇsɪᴅᴇɴᴛ Gᴇᴏʀɢᴇ W. Bᴜsʜ sᴛᴏᴏᴅ ʙᴇʜɪɴᴅ ʜɪs ᴅᴇsᴋ ɪɴ ᴛʜᴇ Oᴠᴀʟ Oꜰꜰɪᴄᴇ, sᴜʀʀᴏᴜɴᴅᴇᴅ ʙʏ reporters and photographers. He had just finished a telephone call with New York Mayor Rudy Giuliani and Governor George Pataki, telling them that the Nation mourned with them and that he would visit New York City the next day. The two days and nights since September 11th had been long, difficult ones. President Bush had visited the Pentagon, where smoke still choked the air and exhausted rescue workers searched for survivors, and told military leaders to be ready. He had convened meetings of the National Security Council, his Cabinet and members of Congress. All of us working at the White House tried to anticipate and prepare for the worst: What if a radioactive device was detonated in an American city? Could the terrorists access and unleash biological, chemical or nuclear weapons?

Like all Americans, reporters in the Oval Office that morning wanted answers: Who was responsible for these acts of terror? Was it safe to fly? And as he prepared for a national prayer service the next morning, what kind of guidance was America's leader asking for himself? "I don't think about myself right now," President Bush replied. "I think about the families, the children. I am a loving guy...." The President's voice cracked; he stopped talking and looked down, struggling to control his emotions. Suddenly, the room felt too small to contain all of the horror and sorrow of the past two days. I looked over at another member of our staff and a reporter, and saw my own tears mirrored in their eyes. The President's voice brought us back to work: "I am also someone, however, who has got a job to do—and I intend to do it." At that moment, in the aftermath of the worst terror attack in American history—with airplanes grounded, the stock market closed, the economy reeling, bodies still being pulled from the rubble—President Bush saw hope. "Through the tears of sadness," he said, "I see an opportunity."

That sentence, that sentiment, captures President Bush and the first four years of his presidency better than any I know. Faced with the evil of the indiscriminate murder of innocents, he saw and seized the opportunity to transform the world for good. He helped the rest of us see that possibility, too. President Bush had always been disciplined, determined and focused on the big picture. During the days and months after September 11th, he became even more intent and strategic. He emerged as a transformative leader determined with every fiber of his being to extend freedom at home and abroad—to make "this young century…liberty's century."

President Bush saw that America's vital interests and our deepest values are one. He made the decision to confront not only terror and terrorists, but also the conditions of oppression and corruption that can give rise to terror and always defy America's founding conviction: that every life has dignity and value, because those are the gifts of our Creator. America would always stand firm, he told us, for the "non-negotiable demands of human dignity: the rule of law; limits on the power of the state; respect for women; respect for private property; and free speech; and equal justice; and religious tolerance." And as the nations of the world worked together to defeat terror, the President said, we could transform individual lives and entire regions; he saw new hope for the cause of peace in the Middle East. America would embrace a forward strategy of freedom, because we know that liberty advances hope, progress and peace for all the world's citizens.

President Bush also championed greater freedom at home. Government should provide not just programs, he said, but a path to greater opportunity, more choices and a better life. His historic education reforms insisted on accountability and results, so that all young people could have the excellent education so vital to participating in the full promise of America. He advocated fundamental reforms of Social Security, Medicare and the tax code, all designed to encourage greater entrepreneurship and ownership. And he knew that the public interest depended on private character, so he supported strong marriages and families, respect for life, and a partnership with the faith-based community and charitable institutions that nurture the human heart and spirit.

The essence of a presidency is often captured in small moments: a bullhorn clasped in one hand as the other encircles a retired firefighter; a fallen policeman's badge, given by a grieving mother, that becomes the symbol of "lives that ended and a task that does not end"; a handshake between the leaders of Britain and the United States, whose shared resolve toppled a threat to world peace and liberated the people of Iraq.

This book is a collection of those moments, captured by the White House photographers, whose work provides an intimate, behind the scenes account of the Bush presidency.

They portray a man of strength and determination, humor and humanity. They reveal a husband, wife and family whose love and respect for each other gives private strength and comfort in the most public of places. They celebrate moments of inspiration and awe, from the mound at Yankee Stadium, where a perfect presidential pitch ignited an ovation that told the world that New York City was back, to the South Lawn of the White House, where the next generation of Americans hits balls from a tee and dreams of perhaps one day returning to serve in the most powerful office in the world. They portray the weight of decisions that only a president can make, and the contributions of the team of people whose work helps guide and inform those decisions. They remind us of the horrors and victories of the last century and their terrible costs, and challenge us with the possibility of writing a new story of American leadership for a more hopeful and more peaceful world.

Perhaps most of all, they celebrate freedom and honor service. For as they chronicle four years of the presidency, these photos also tell the story of an America whose young men and women still volunteer their lives to the larger cause of freedom. Through their service, and the words of the President: "America, in this young century, proclaims liberty throughout all the world, and to all the inhabitants thereof. Renewed in our strength—tested, but not weary—we are ready for the greatest achievements in the history of freedom."

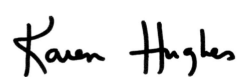

"THROUGH MUCH OF THE LAST CENTURY, America's faith in freedom and democracy was a rock in a raging sea. Now it is a seed upon the wind, taking root in many nations. Our democratic faith is more than the creed of our country, it is the inborn hope of our humanity, an ideal we carry but do not own, a trust we bear and pass along. And even after nearly 225 years, we have a long way yet to travel."

—*President George W. Bush,*
Inaugural Address,
Washington, D.C.,
January 20, 2001

President-elect George W. Bush and Laura Bush are greeted by President Bill Clinton and Hillary Rodham Clinton at the North Portico of the White House. The meeting was part of an orderly transition of power that would continue later in the day with the official Inauguration Ceremony, and stands as a great symbol of the American democratic system. *January 20, 2001*

Sitting in the Oval Office for the first time as President, George W. Bush shares a moment with his father, former President George H. W. Bush. Of the 43 American presidents, only two—John Quincy Adams and George W. Bush—have followed their fathers into the Nation's highest office.
January 20, 2001

George H. W. and Barbara Bush return to the South Lawn for a walk with their son, inaugurated eight days earlier as President of the United States.
January 28, 2001

President Bush and Vice President Cheney lead an Oval Office discussion on the economy with senior members of the domestic policy staff.
January 6, 2003

President Bush uses a quiet moment in the Oval Office to prepare for a meeting with Prime Minister Yoshiro Mori of Japan. Mori was one of the first world leaders to meet with President Bush.
March 19, 2001

President Bush reflects during a telephone conversation with Egyptian President Hosni Mubarak. Regular contact with heads of state around the world is a constant requirement for the President of the United States.
January 28, 2002

President Bush and Senator Edward Kennedy meet to discuss the President's No Child Left Behind initiative.
January 23, 2001

Barney, a Scottish Terrier given to the Bush family from Environmental Protection Agency Administrator Christine Todd Whitman, looks out onto the South Lawn from the Oval Office.
May 14, 2003

President and Mrs. Bush do some last-minute tidying while awaiting the arrival of White House curators and decorators. The President selected the "Resolute" desk, made from timbers from the HMS *Resolute*, an abandoned British ship. He is the 22nd President to use the desk since it was given to the White House in 1880 by Queen Victoria of England.
January 30, 2002

Mrs. Bush goes for a stroll through the Rose Garden with dogs Barney and Spot.
February 22, 2001

President Bush shows his pitching form on the South Lawn in preparation for throwing out the first pitch on opening day of the 2001 baseball season.
April 3, 2001

After spending time at their ranch in Crawford, Texas, President and Mrs. Bush walk to Air Force One. The specially configured Boeing 747 is capable of flying halfway around the world without refueling, and is outfitted with communications equipment that allow the President and his staff to work aloft while maintaining contact with anyone in the world. *June 25, 2001*

"I believe that God has planted in every human heart the desire to live in freedom. And even when that desire is crushed by tyranny for decades, it will rise again."

President and Mrs. Bush are greeted by troops outside the chapel at Camp Bondsteel in Kosovo.
July 24, 2001

"OUR DUTY IS TO USE THE LAND WELL, and sometimes, not to use it at all. This is our responsibility as citizens; but, more than that, it is our calling as stewards of the Earth. Good stewardship of the environment is not just a personal responsibility, it is a public value. Americans are united in the belief that we must preserve our natural heritage and safeguard the land around us."

—*President George W. Bush,*
Sequoia National Park,
California,
May 30, 2001

U.S. Park Rangers point out to the President and Interior Secretary Gale Norton some of the natural formations at Sequoia National Park. President Bush is the first chief executive to visit the park while in office.
May 30, 2001

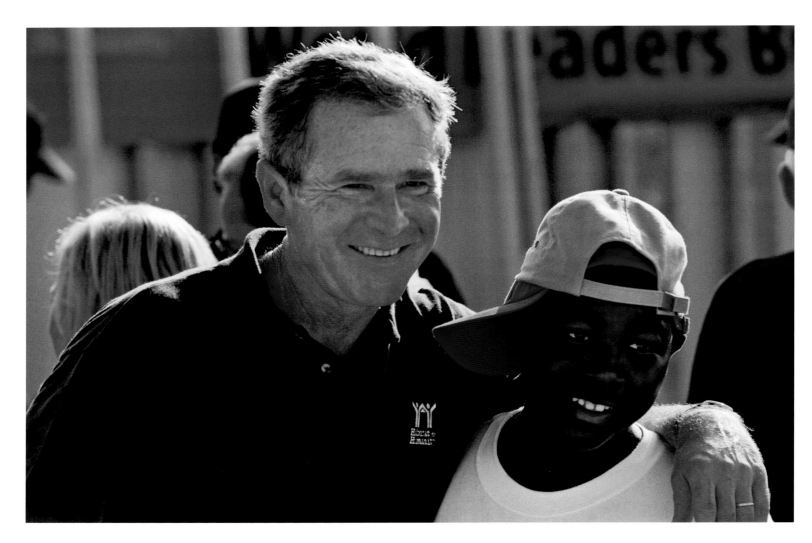

The President joins Habitat for Humanity volunteers to build a home in Waco, Texas. Working with the President that day was one of the home's future residents, Edwin "Bubba" Evans.
August 8, 2001

President Bush helps Habitat for Humanity volunteers build the wall of a home for the Rodriguez family in Tampa, Florida. During his first State of the Union Address following the 9/11 attacks, President Bush announced the creation of USA Freedom Corps, a service organization with goals of rebuilding communities and extending American compassion and goodwill. *June 5, 2001*

Behind the wheel of his pickup truck, President Bush drives around his ranch in central Texas. The 1,600-acre ranch includes a lake, a waterfall, a canyon, and meadows where cattle and deer graze.
August 7, 2001

President Bush and Spanish President José María Aznar walk through a canyon at the ranch. The President has hosted world leaders from a number of countries at his Texas home, including those of Australia, Italy, Japan, Mexico, Russia, Saudi Arabia and the United Kingdom.
February 22, 2003

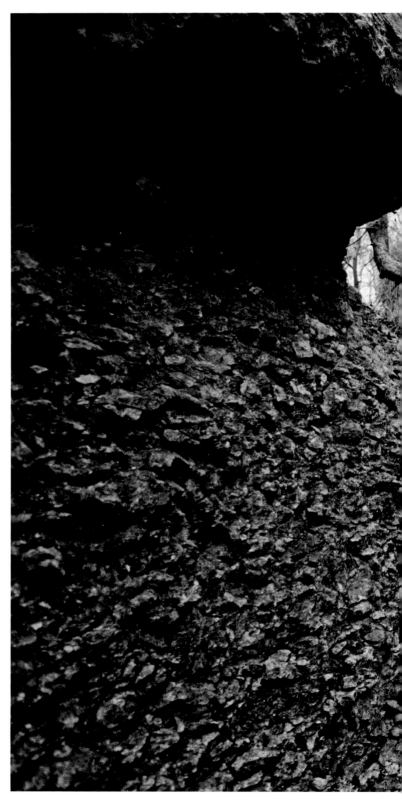

"We have a duty in our country to make sure our land is preserved, our air is clean, and our water is pure."

President Bush collects brush to be burned on his sprawling Texas ranch. The Bush family home in central Texas has become an important secondary base of operations for the President, as was President Dwight D. Eisenhower's farm in Gettysburg, Pennsylvania, and President Ronald Reagan's ranch in California.

December 29, 2001

President Bush takes a walk amid the colorful wildflowers that blanket his ranch in Crawford, Texas. The President purchased the ranch in 1999, when he was Governor of Texas.
May 23, 2003

Mrs. Bush walks with her niece
through the fog at Camp David,
in the mountains of Maryland
near Washington, D.C. Camp
David gives Presidents' families a peaceful haven for short
weekend visits.
April 8, 2001

President and Mrs. Bush share
a private moment during a
church service at Evergreen
Chapel, Camp David.
April 8, 2001

"I WANT YOU ALL TO KNOW THAT AMERICA today...is on bended knee in prayer for the people whose lives were lost here, for the workers who work here, for the families who mourn. This Nation stands with the good people of New York City, and New Jersey and Connecticut, as we mourn the loss of thousands of our citizens.... I can hear you. The rest of the world hears you. And the people who knocked these buildings down will hear all of us soon."

— *President George W. Bush,*
addressing rescue workers
gathered at Ground Zero,
New York City,
September 14, 2001

Three days after the 9/11 attacks, President Bush stands beside retired New York City firefighter Bob Beckwith and others at the ruins of the World Trade Center.
September 14, 2001

The President had been reading to a fourth-grade class when White House Chief of Staff Andrew Card interrupted to tell the Commander in Chief, "America is under attack." A classroom at Emma E. Booker Elementary School in Sarasota, Florida, was quickly transformed into a presidential command center. *September 11, 2001*

On the day of the attacks, the
President maintains communica-
tion with Vice President Cheney,
key members of the Cabinet, and
his national command staff while
onboard Air Force One.
September 11, 2001

Vice President Cheney and
senior staff members witness
the collapse of the World Trade
Center from the Presidential
Emergency Operations Center.
September 11, 2001

During a Cabinet Room meeting with the National Security Council the day after the 9/11 attacks, President Bush stated how the country would respond. "The United States of America will use all our resources to conquer this enemy," he told them. "We will rally the world. We will be patient, we will be focused, and we will be steadfast in our determination."
September 12, 2001

The President visits with civilian, military relief and rescue workers at the Pentagon to express the Nation's thanks. Many of the rescue workers had driven all night to help in the effort.
September 12, 2001

"This battle will take time and resolve.
But make no mistake about it: We will win."

" **O**N THIS NATIONAL DAY OF PRAYER and remembrance, we ask almighty God to watch over our nation and grant us patience and resolve in all that is to come. We pray that he will comfort and console those who now walk in sorrow. We thank him for each life we now must mourn, and the promise of a life to come."

—President George W. Bush,
National Cathedral,
Washington, D.C.,
September 14, 2001

National and world leaders, including President George W. Bush and former presidents Bush, Carter, Clinton, and Ford, attend a memorial service at the National Cathedral for victims of the terrorist attacks. President Bush had declared September 14, 2001, to be a National Day of Prayer and Remembrance, and encouraged all people to join in the solemn observances.
September 14, 2001

Addressing a joint session of Congress, President Bush holds up the police shield of George Howard, which was given to the President by Howard's mother as a memorial to her son and those who died at the World Trade Center trying to save others.
September 20, 2001

President Bush talks with Arlene Howard after she presented him with the police badge worn by her late son. Following the 9/11 attacks, the President spent much of his time meeting with and consoling victims' families.
September 14, 2001

"I will not forget this wound to our country or those who inflicted it. I will not yield; I will not rest; I will not relent in waging this struggle for freedom and security for the American people."

FBI Director Robert Mueller, CIA Director George Tenet, Attorney General John Ashcroft, and Homeland Security Director Tom Ridge confer in a White House strategy meeting. *October 29, 2001*

Just weeks after the 9/11 attacks, President Bush meets with National Security Advisor Condoleezza Rice, Chief of Staff Andrew Card, and CIA Director George Tenet at Camp David. *September 29, 2001*

On the first anniversary of the terrorist attacks, President and Mrs. Bush walk down the ramp to Ground Zero in New York City, where they would lay a wreath at the site of the World Trade Center to commemorate those who died there.
September 11, 2002

President and Mrs. Bush light
a candle at St. John's Episcopal
Church in Washington, D.C.,
during a private service commem-
orating the one-year anniversary
of the terrorist attacks.
September 11, 2002

"MY FAITH PLAYS A BIG PART IN MY LIFE…IT'S VERY personal. I pray for strength. I pray for wisdom. I pray for troops in harm's way. I pray for my family. I pray for my little girls. But I'm mindful in a free society that people can worship if they want to or not. You're equally an American if you choose to worship an almighty and if you choose not to."

— *President George W. Bush,*
October 13, 2004

President and Mrs. Bush participate
in a wreath-laying ceremony in
memory of the victims of Flight 93,
which crashed on September 11
in Somerset County, Pennsylvania.
September 12, 2002

A contemplative moment for the President on the grounds of the White House, who on this day announced he was sending Peace Corps workers to Afghanistan for the first time since 1979.
February 15, 2002

Previous page: As the President departs the White House in the presidential helicopter, Marine One, a crowd gathers on the South Lawn to wish him well. American flags and other symbols of patriotism surged in popularity after the 9/11 attacks. *September 21, 2001*

Tee-ball games are a regularly scheduled event on summer Sunday afternoons on the White House lawn. President Bush is a lifelong baseball fan and former Major League Baseball executive. *June 23, 2002*

Just weeks after the attacks of September 11, the President takes to the mound to throw out the first pitch at Yankee Stadium in the 2001 World Series. The pitch went right down the middle for a strike. *October 30, 2001*

U.S. Attorney General Alberto
Gonzales *(at left)* listens to
President Bush's remarks at the
fifteenth annual United States
Hispanic Chamber of Commerce
Legislative Conference in
Washington, D.C.
April 20, 2005

At a White House event
celebrating National Hispanic
Heritage Month, President
Bush signs an executive order
establishing the President's
Advisory Commission on
Educational Excellence for
Hispanic Americans.
October 12, 2001

The President tours a USA Industries manufacturing plant in Bay Shore, New York, where he later discussed economic policies with a panel of employees from the factory. One of the President's main priorities is to continue to create a cultural and economic environment where businesses can flourish, and every American who wants a good job can find one.
March 11, 2004

President Bush talks with neighbors in the city of Crawford, Texas, a few miles from his ranch. "When I'm not in Washington, there's a pretty good chance you'll find me on our place in Crawford," the President has said.
August 19, 2003

President Bush consoles a resident of Punta Gorda, Florida, in the aftermath of Hurricane Charley.
August 15, 2004

Mrs. Bush visits with Red Cross staff at a community center that was turned into a disaster relief center following the damaging hurricanes in Vero Beach, Florida.
October 1, 2004

On Earth Day, the President
visits a park in the Adirondack
Mountains of upstate New York.
April 22, 2002

President Bush visits the Islamic
Center of Washington, D.C.,
telling community leaders, "The
face of terror is not the true
faith of Islam. That's not what
Islam is all about. Islam is peace."
September 17, 2001

Mrs. Bush's meeting with female Afghan teachers at the White House brought attention to the progress of women in that country following the defeat of the Taliban. In a society where girls were previously not allowed to attend school, women are now teachers.
December 4, 2002

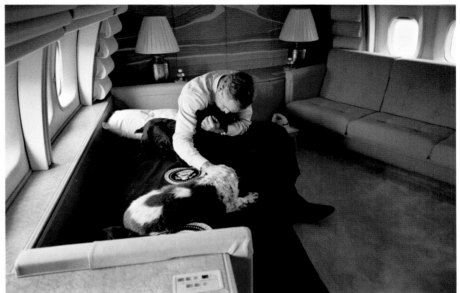

In the final days of the 2004 campaign, the President and his staff take a few minutes to relax in the conference room aboard Air Force One as they fly from Albuquerque to Dallas.
November 1, 2004

The President shows his appreciation to some of his loyal supporters while aboard Air Force One.
February 20, 2003

Vice President and Mrs. Cheney
enjoy a family get-together over
Easter weekend at the official
Vice Presidential residence at the
Naval Observatory *(above)*.
On a sundial sculpture on the
Observatory lawn, the Vice
President follows in the footsteps
of his granddaughter Katie, while
her sisters, Elizabeth and Grace,
her mother, Liz, and Mrs. Cheney
look on *(right)*.
April 20, 2003

Like American mothers everywhere, Mrs. Bush is happiest spending Thanksgiving surrounded by family. Here the clan gathers at Camp David for the holiday.
November 22, 2001

President Bush and his brother
Marvin head up friendly rival
teams for a family tournament
at the White House bowling
alley on Christmas Day.
December 25, 2001

"TODAY BEGINS A NEW ERA, A NEW TIME IN PUBLIC education in our country. As of this hour, America's schools will be on a new path of reform, and a new path of results. Our schools will have higher expectations. We believe every child can learn. Our schools will have greater resources to help meet those goals. Parents will have more information about the schools, and more say in how their children are educated. From this day forward, all students will have a better chance to learn, to excel and to live out their dreams."

—*President George W. Bush,*
on the signing of the
No Child Left Behind Act,
Hamilton, Ohio,
January 8, 2002

President Bush visits with students at the B.W. Tinker School in Waterbury, Connecticut, where he reminded Americans that his No Child Left Behind initiative will increase the performance of students in the critical areas of reading, math, and science.
April 18, 2001

Lynne Cheney reads from her book *America: A Patriotic Primer* at the White House Easter Egg Roll. Proceeds from Mrs. Cheney's children's books are used to fund the James Madison Book Award Fund, which presents an annual award to the book that best promotes knowledge and understanding of American history to young people.
April 21, 2003

Mrs. Bush shares storytime with students at Public School 41 in New York City. A former teacher and librarian, Mrs. Bush is an important ally in the President's efforts to ensure that every child receives a quality education.
September 25, 2001

Mrs. Bush hugs Sydney Anderson, 11, as President Bush greets the child's mother, Sandy, the wife of Space Shuttle *Columbia* Payload Commander Lieutenant Colonel Michael Anderson, during a visit by the families of the Space Shuttle crew to the Oval Office. Lieutenant Colonel Anderson and the other crew members were killed in the *Columbia* accident a month earlier.
March 7, 2003

President and Mrs. Bush spend time with Nancy Reagan at Blair House on the eve of President Ronald Reagan's funeral.
June 10, 2004

Vice President Cheney confers with National Security Advisor Condoleezza Rice in the Red Room at the White House. Dr. Rice would later be appointed by the President to be Secretary of State. *March 19, 2003*

"The dangers to our country and the world will be overcome. We will pass through this time of peril and carry on the work of peace."

President Bush confers with Vice President Cheney and Secretary of Defense Donald Rumsfeld outside the Oval Office *(top)* and with his national security and communications advisors *(bottom)* shortly after authorizing military operations in Iraq. *March 19, 2003*

President Bush spends some time alone before his address to the Nation announcing the beginning of Operation Iraqi Freedom. *March 19, 2003*

"THIS YOUNG CENTURY WILL BE LIBERTY'S century. By promoting liberty abroad, we will build a safer world. By encouraging liberty at home, we will build a more hopeful America. Like generations before us, we have a calling from beyond the stars to stand for freedom. This is the everlasting dream of America."

— *President George W. Bush,*
Republican National Convention,
New York City,
September 2, 2004

President Bush walks onstage to honor military personnel and their families at Fort Stewart, Georgia.
September 12, 2003

Mrs. Bush visits members of the 101st Airborne at Fort Campbell, Kentucky. The division, known as the Screaming Eagles, has served in World War II, Vietnam, and the Balkans.
November 21, 2001

President Bush attends the U.S. Citizenship Ceremony for wounded Marine Corps Lance Corporal O. J. Santamaria at the National Naval Medical Center in Bethesda, Maryland.
April 11, 2003

President George W. Bush gets
a warm reception from soldiers
at MacDill Air Force Base in
Tampa, Florida.
March 26, 2003

"America counts on the men and women who have stepped forward as volunteers in the cause of freedom....Thank you for the credit and honor you bring to our country every day."

As dusk begins to settle over Iraq, President Bush spends the final moments of his historic flight with the pilots of Air Force One *(left)* as they begin their descent into Baghdad. Only a handful of White House staff accompanied the President on his secret mission to show support for America's military men and women. After his surprise arrival, President Bush jumps into the chow line *(above)* to serve Thanksgiving dinner to troops at the Bob Hope Dining Facility.
November 27, 2003

Mr President,

Iraq is sovereign. Letter was passed from Bremer at 10:26 AM Iraq time —

Condi

Let Freedom Reign!

While attending the opening session of a NATO Summit in Istanbul, Turkey, President Bush was notified (via a handwritten note from National Security Advisor Condoleezza Rice) that sovereignty had been returned to the Iraqi people. President Bush responds by writing "Let Freedom Reign!" on the note *(above)*, and shaking hands with British Prime Minister Tony Blair *(right)*.
June 28, 2004

"THE ADVANCE OF FREEDOM IS THE CALLING of our time; it is the calling of our country. From the Fourteen Points to the Four Freedoms... America has put our power at the service of principle. We believe that liberty is the design of nature; we believe that liberty is the direction of history. We believe that human fulfillment and excellence come in the responsible exercise of liberty. And we believe that freedom—the freedom we prize—is not for us alone, it is the right and the capacity of all mankind."

*—President George W. Bush,
20th Anniversary of the National
Endowment for Democracy,
Washington, D.C.,
November 6, 2003*

Honoring a previous generation of American heroes, President and Mrs. Bush visit the Normandy American Cemetery in Colleville-sur-Mer, France. *May 27, 2002*

A crowd in Vilnius, Lithuania, wait for President Bush and Lithuanian President Valdas Adamkus. "You have known cruel oppression and withstood it," President Bush told them, referring to the Soviet occupation of the country in the last century. "You were held captive by an empire and you outlived it. And because you have paid its cost, you know the value of human freedom."
November 23, 2002

President Bush walks onstage with Romanian President Ion Iliescu prior to addressing thousands gathered in Bucharest, Romania's Revolution Square, the site of the 1989 revolt that toppled Communist rule.
November 23, 2002

Together with Senegalese President Abdoulaye Wade and Viviane Wade, President and Mrs. Bush tour the House of Slaves on Goree Island, off the coast of Dakar, Senegal.
July 8, 2003

President Bush makes a point to Russian President Vladimir Putin at the G8 Summit in Italy. The member nations of the G8—Canada, France, Germany, Italy, Japan, Russia, the United Kingdom, and the United States—meet yearly to discuss international issues.
July 22, 2001

"There's a way to accomplish the separation of church and state, and at the same time, accomplish the social objective of having America become a hopeful place, and a loving place."

After a meeting in Jacksonville, Florida, during the 2000 presidential campaign, then-Texas Governor George W. Bush speaks with the Reverend Billy Graham.
November 5, 2000

During their first meeting, Pope John Paul II and President Bush look out over Lake Albano at the pontiff's summer residence in Castel Gandolfo near Rome.
July 23, 2001

President and Mrs. Bush place a rose
at the end of the railroad tracks at
the site of the Auschwitz-Birkenau
concentration camp in Oswiecim,
Poland. The majority of the Jews
deported to Auschwitz during the Nazi
occupation of Poland in World War II
were killed in the gas chambers of the
Auschwitz-Birkenau camp.
May 31, 2003

*"By the unselfish dedication of Americans in uniform,
people in our own country and in lands far away can live
in freedom and know the peace that freedom brings."*

President Bush takes a moment to reflect prior to his participation in a Memorial Day ceremony at Arlington National Cemetery. In his address, he said, "Today we honor the men and women who have worn the Nation's uniform and were last seen on duty." *May 26, 2003*

President Bush talks with World War II veterans and brothers Jose Ramos Chavez and Joe Diego Chavez at a breakfast hosted by Veterans Affairs Secretary Anthony Principi in the Executive Dining Room at the White House. Jose was part of the D-Day landings at Normandy, and Joe served in both the Atlantic and Pacific theaters. *May 28, 2004*

President Bush meets with Prime
Minister Ariel Sharon of Israel
(at left), and Prime Minister
Mahmoud Abbas of the Palestinian
Authority at the Red Sea Summit
in Aqaba, Jordan.
June 4, 2003

With freedom and democracy in the Middle East as a principal part of the agenda at the G8 Summit in Sea Island, Georgia, President Bush meets with Ghazi al-Yawer, President of the Interim Government of Iraq.
June 9, 2004

President Bush walks on the beach with other world leaders at the Sea Island G8 Summit. The President said, "The nations of the G8 recognize our special responsibility to help the people of the Middle East achieve the progress they seek. And here at Sea Island, we pledged that our nations will help further the causes of freedom and reform."
June 9, 2004

President Bush greets Hamid Karzai—then-Chairman of the Afghan Interim Authority—in the Oval Office. "Chairman Karzai is a determined leader, and his government reflects the hopes of all Afghans for a new and better future; a future free from terror, free from war, and free from want," the President said.
January 28, 2002

Vice President Cheney and President Hamid Karzai, Afghanistan's first democratically elected head of state, answer questions from the press at the Presidential Palace in Kabul, Afghanistan.
December 7, 2004

"THE MAN WHO SITS IN THE OVAL OFFICE will set the course of the war on terror and the direction of our economy. The security and prosperity of America are at stake. Our course is clear. In the next four years, we'll keep our enemies on the run, and extend the frontiers of liberty. In the next four years, we'll help more Americans to find their opportunities in a changing economy. In the next four years, we will stand for the values that make us a good and decent country."

—*President George W. Bush,*
Republican Governors Association,
Washington, D.C.,
February 23, 2004

A crowd in Kalamazoo, Michigan, greets President Bush during his first bus tour of the 2004 campaign.
May 3, 2004

A crowd of hands reaches out to President Bush during a rally at Parkersburg High School in West Virginia. *September 5, 2004*

President Bush poses for a picture with a soldier's son at Fort Polk, Louisiana. *February 17, 2004*

The President gets a congratu-
latory hug from his wife and
daughters following his third
and final presidential debate
with Senator John Kerry in
Tempe, Arizona.
October 13, 2004

The President and Laura Bush
walk hand-in-hand amid a
chorus of cheers and confetti
after the President's address at
the 2004 Republican National
Convention at Madison Square
Garden in New York City.
September 2, 2004

Supporters cheer President Bush during a rally at the Coconut Grove Expo Center in Miami, Florida *(top).* *October 31, 2004*

President Bush gets a big welcome from a crowd in Missouri *(above).* *September 6, 2004*

Thousands of people fill the Troy Public Square to hear President Bush address a rally in Troy, Ohio.
August 28, 2004

Children greet President
Bush as he arrives aboard his
campaign bus in Pottstown,
Pennsylvania.
July 9, 2004

President Bush walks with
Karl Rove, Senior Advisor
to the President, along the
colonnade in the Rose Garden.
January 27, 2003

Gathering in the Family Dining
Room at the White House, the
President's family and staff
monitor the news as election
returns come in.
November 2, 2004

In the early morning hours after the election, President and Mrs. Bush share a private moment. The President's opponent, Senator John Kerry, called him to concede later that day.
November 3, 2004

"We are not this story's author, who fills time and eternity with his purpose. Yet his purpose is achieved in our duty.... This work continues. This story goes on. And an angel still rides in the whirlwind and directs this storm."

President Bush, Vice President Cheney, and their families attend prayer services at St. John's Episcopal Church in Washington, D.C., on inauguration day.
January 20, 2005

"FROM ALL OF YOU, I HAVE ASKED patience in the hard task of securing America, which you have granted in good measure. Our country has accepted obligations that are difficult to fulfill, and would be dishonorable to abandon. Yet, because we have acted in the great liberating tradition of this nation, tens of millions have achieved their freedom."

— *President George W. Bush,
Inaugural Address,
Washington, D.C.,
January 20, 2005*

A sea of onlookers surrounds the West Steps of the U.S. Capitol to witness the second swearing-in ceremony of President George W. Bush. *January 20, 2005*

President George W. Bush is sworn in to a second term of office by Chief Justice of the United States William H. Rehnquist. *January 20, 2005*

President Bush and Vice President Cheney shake hands following their second inauguration. *January 20, 2005*

As the University of Texas marching band passes by the Presidential reviewing stand, Texans salute the musicians with the school's familiar "Hook 'em Horns" hand sign.
January 20, 2005

Thousands of people line the streets of Washington to watch the Inaugural Parade. President and Mrs. Bush watched as more than 10,000 participants from across the country marched in the parade.
January 20, 2005

President Bush pulls on his cowboy boots in preparation for the Texas State Society's Black Tie and Boots Ball, an unconventional yet formal gala dating back 20 years. With a Texan in the White House, the event has become the hottest ticket in town.
January 19, 2005

President Bush, Vice President
Cheney, and their families
take their places backstage at
the Black Tie and Boots Ball.
January 19, 2005

After they had each danced with a military partner, President and Mrs. Bush reunite on the dance floor of the Commander-in-Chief Ball, which was introduced this year to honor troops just returning from or about to be deployed to Afghanistan and Iraq. The First Couple visited a total of nine official Inaugural Balls that evening to show their appreciation to and share the celebration with their many supporters.

January 20, 2005

The Inaugural Address

January 20, 2005

O N THIS DAY, PRESCRIBED BY LAW AND MARKED BY CEREMONY, WE celebrate the durable wisdom of our Constitution, and recall the deep commitments that unite our country. I am grateful for the honor of this hour, mindful of the consequential times in which we live, and determined to fulfill the oath that I have sworn and you have witnessed.

At this second gathering, our duties are defined not by the words I use, but by the history we have seen together. For a half-century, America defended our own freedom by standing watch on distant borders. After the shipwreck of communism came years of relative quiet, years of repose, years of sabbatical—and then there came a day of fire.

We have seen our vulnerability—and we have seen its deepest source. For as long as whole regions of the world simmer in resentment and tyranny—prone to ideologies that feed hatred and excuse murder—violence will gather, and multiply in destructive power, and cross the most defended borders, and raise a mortal threat. There is only one force of history that can break the reign of hatred and resentment, and expose the pretensions of tyrants, and reward the hopes of the decent and tolerant, and that is the force of human freedom.

We are led, by events and common sense, to one conclusion: The survival of liberty in our land increasingly depends on the success of liberty in other lands. The best hope for peace in our world is the expansion of freedom in all the world.

America's vital interests and our deepest beliefs are now one. From the day of our Founding, we have proclaimed that every man and woman on this earth has rights, and dignity, and matchless value, because they bear the image of the Maker of Heaven and Earth. Across the generations we have proclaimed the imperative of self-government, because no one is fit to be a master, and no one deserves to be a slave. Advancing these ideals is the mission that created our Nation. It is the honorable achievement of our fathers. Now it is the urgent requirement of our nation's security, and the calling of our time.

So it is the policy of the United States to seek and support the growth of democratic movements and institutions in every nation and culture, with the ultimate goal of ending tyranny in our world.

This is not primarily the task of arms, though we will defend ourselves and our friends by force of arms when necessary. Freedom, by its nature, must be chosen, and defended by citizens, and sustained by the rule of law and the protection of minorities. And when the soul of a nation finally speaks, the institutions that arise may reflect customs and traditions very different from our own. America will not impose our own style of government on the unwilling. Our goal instead is to help others find their own voice, attain their own freedom, and make their own way.

The great objective of ending tyranny is the concentrated work of generations. The difficulty of the task is no excuse for avoiding it. America's influence is not unlimited, but fortunately for the oppressed, America's influence is considerable, and we will use it confidently in freedom's cause.

My most solemn duty is to protect this nation and its people against further attacks and emerging threats. Some have unwisely chosen to test America's resolve, and have found it firm.

We will persistently clarify the choice before every ruler and every nation: The moral choice between oppression, which is always wrong, and freedom, which is eternally right. America will not pretend that jailed dissidents prefer their chains, or that women welcome humiliation and servitude, or that any human being aspires to live at the mercy of bullies.

We will encourage reform in other governments by making clear that success in our relations will require the decent treatment of their own people. America's belief in human dignity will guide our policies, yet rights must be more than the grudging concessions of dictators; they are secured by free dissent and the participation of the governed. In the long run, there is no justice without freedom, and there can be no human rights without human liberty.

Some, I know, have questioned the global appeal of liberty—though this time in history, four decades defined by the swiftest advance of freedom ever seen, is an odd time for doubt. Americans, of all people, should never be surprised by the power of our ideals. Eventually, the call of freedom comes to every mind and every soul. We do not accept the existence of permanent tyranny because we do not accept the possibility of permanent slavery. Liberty will come to those who love it.

Today, America speaks anew to the peoples of the world:

All who live in tyranny and hopelessness can know: the United States will not ignore your oppression, or excuse your oppressors. When you stand for your liberty, we will stand with you.

Democratic reformers facing repression, prison, or exile can know: America sees you for who you are—the future leaders of your free country.

The rulers of outlaw regimes can know that we still believe as Abraham Lincoln did: "Those who deny freedom to others deserve it not for themselves; and, under the rule of a just God, cannot long retain it."

The leaders of governments with long habits of control need to know: To serve your people you must learn to trust them. Start on this journey of progress and justice, and America will walk at your side.

And all the allies of the United States can know: we honor your friendship, we rely on your counsel, and we depend on your help. Division among free nations is a primary goal of freedom's enemies. The concerted effort of free nations to promote democracy is a prelude to our enemies' defeat.

Today, I also speak anew to my fellow citizens:

From all of you, I have asked patience in the hard task of securing America, which you have granted in good measure. Our country has accepted obligations that are difficult to fulfill, and would be dishonorable to abandon. Yet because we have acted in the great liberating tradition of this nation, tens of millions have achieved their freedom. And as hope kindles hope, millions more will find it. By our efforts, we have lit a fire as well—a fire in the minds of men. It warms those who feel its power, it burns those who fight its progress, and one day this untamed fire of freedom will reach the darkest corners of our world.

A few Americans have accepted the hardest duties in this cause—in the quiet work of intelligence and diplomacy...the idealistic work of helping raise up free governments...the dangerous and necessary work of fighting our enemies. Some have shown their devotion to our country in deaths that honored their whole lives—and we will always honor their names and their sacrifice.

All Americans have witnessed this idealism, and some for the first time. I ask our youngest citizens to believe the evidence of your eyes. You have seen duty and allegiance in the determined faces of our soldiers. You have seen that life is fragile, and evil is real, and courage triumphs. Make the choice to serve in a cause larger than your wants, larger than yourself—and in your days you will add not just to the wealth of our country, but to its character.

America has need of idealism and courage, because we have essential work at home—the unfinished work of American freedom. In a world moving toward liberty, we are determined to show the meaning and promise of liberty.

In America's ideal of freedom, citizens find the dignity and security of economic independence, instead of laboring on the edge of subsistence. This is the broader definition of liberty that motivated the Homestead Act, the Social Security Act, and the GI Bill of Rights. And now we will extend this vision by reforming great institutions to serve the needs of our time. To give every American a stake in the promise and future of our country, we will bring the highest standards to our schools, and build an ownership society. We will widen the ownership of homes and businesses, retirement savings and health insurance—preparing our people for the challenges of life in a free society. By making every citizen an agent of his or her own destiny, we will give our fellow Americans greater freedom from want and fear, and make our society more prosperous and just and equal.

In America's ideal of freedom, the public interest depends on private character—on integrity, and tolerance toward others, and the rule of conscience in our own lives. Self-government relies, in the end, on the governing of the self. That edifice of character is built in families, supported by communities with standards, and sustained in our national life by the truths of Sinai, the Sermon on the Mount, the words of the Koran, and the varied faiths of our people. Americans move forward in every generation by reaffirming all that is good and true that came before—ideals of justice and conduct that are the same yesterday, today, and forever.

In America's ideal of freedom, the exercise of rights is ennobled by service, and mercy, and a heart for the weak. Liberty for all does not mean independence from one another. Our nation relies on men and women who look after a neighbor and surround the lost with love. Americans, at our best, value the life we see in one another, and must always remember that even the unwanted have worth. And our country must abandon all the habits of racism, because we cannot carry the message of freedom and the baggage of bigotry at the same time.

From the perspective of a single day, including this day of dedication, the issues and questions before our country are many. From the viewpoint of centuries, the questions that come to us are narrowed and few. Did our generation advance the cause of freedom? And did our character bring credit to that cause?

These questions that judge us also unite us, because Americans of every party and background, Americans by choice and by birth, are bound to one another in the cause of freedom. We have known divisions, which must be healed to move forward in great purposes—and I will strive in good faith to heal them. Yet those divisions do not define America. We felt the unity and fellowship of our nation when freedom came under attack, and our response came like a single hand over a single heart. And we can feel that same unity and pride whenever America acts for good, and the victims of disaster are given hope, and the unjust encounter justice, and the captives are set free.

We go forward with complete confidence in the eventual triumph of freedom. Not because history runs on the wheels of inevitability; it is human choices that move events. Not because we consider ourselves a chosen nation; God moves and chooses as He wills. We have confidence because freedom is the permanent hope of mankind, the hunger in dark places, the longing of the soul. When our Founders declared a new order of the ages; when soldiers died in wave upon wave for a union based on liberty; when citizens marched in peaceful outrage under the banner "Freedom Now"—they were acting on an ancient hope that is meant to be fulfilled. History has an ebb and flow of justice, but history also has a visible direction, set by liberty and the Author of Liberty.

When the Declaration of Independence was first read in public and the Liberty Bell was sounded in celebration, a witness said, "It rang as if it meant something." In our time it means something still. America, in this young century, proclaims liberty throughout all the world, and to all the inhabitants thereof. Renewed in our strength—tested, but not weary— we are ready for the greatest achievements in the history of freedom.

May God bless you, and may He watch over the United States of America.

—President George W. Bush

55th PRESIDENTIAL INAUGURAL COMMITTEE

EXECUTIVE COMMITTEE

Co-Chairmen
Garbrielle and Mercer Reynolds
Katherine and William O. Dewitt, Jr.
Bradford M. Freeman

Chairman
Jeanne L. Phillips

Executive Director
Greg Jenkins

Finance Chairman
Nancy Kinder

Honorary Finance Chairman
Al Hoffman

HONORARY COMMITTEE

Mr. Duane W. Acklie
The Honorable Tim Babcock
The Honorable Gilbert R. Baker
Ms. Leslie Gromis Baker
Mr. Jim Barnett
Mr. G. Hunter Bates
Ms. Carmen Bermudez
Mr. John E. Binkley
Mr. Ferrell Blount
Mr. Donald "Boysie" Bollinger
Mr. Jack H. Brier
Mrs. Patricia Brister
Mr. Will Brooke
Mrs. Mary Buestrin
Mrs. De Byerly
Mr. Joseph A. Cannon
Mr. Charles Cawley
Representative Marvin Childers
Mrs. Stephanie H. Chivers
The Honorable Peter Cianchette
The Honorable Jo Ann Davidson
Mr. James O. Donnelly
Mr. Robert M. "Mike" Duncan
Ms. Dorothy Early
Mr. Lewis M. Eisenberg
Mr. Warren K. Erdman
Ms. Nancy J. Ernaut
Mr. Tom Everist
Mr. P. Robert Fanin
Mrs. Elizabeth Walker Field

Ms. Julie Finley
Mr. Thomas C. Foley
Representative Galen Fox
Mr. Ronald L. Fox
Mr. David F. Girard-diCarlo
The Honorable
Brian Paul Golden
Mrs. Kate Obenshain Griffin
Ms. Jean Ann Harcourt
Mr. James H. Harless
The Honorable Paul C. Harris
Mrs. Miriam Hellreich
Mrs. Patricia L. Herbold
Mr. Michael R. Hightower
Mayor Jerry N. Hruby
Mr. Al Hubbard
The Honorable Marilyn L. Huston
Mrs. Martha W. Jenkins
Mr. Mark A. Kahrs
Mr. Robert K. Kjellander
Mr. James R. Klauser
Mr. C. Michael Kojaian
Mr. David Kramer
Mr. David Kustoff
Mr. James R. Lowe
Mr. Robert A. Martinez
Mr. Mike McKay
Mrs. Carolyn D. Meadows
Ms. Patricia L. Morgan
Mrs. Terry Neese

Mrs. Connie Nicholas
Mr. Gerald L. Parski
The Honorable
Joseph Carlton Petrone
Mr. George J. Puentes
Mrs. Paulette L. Pyle
Mr. Clarke T. Reed
Mr. Mario A. Rodriguez
Mr. David M. Roederer
Mr. Raul R. Romero
Mr. Randy Ruedrich
Mrs. Rhonda M. Rutledge
Mr. John A. Sanchez
Mr. Brian Sandoval
Mrs. Mary A. Smith
Mrs. Dorothy W. Stapleton
The Honorable Michael Steele
Wayne Stenehjem
The Honorable Susan A. Story
Mr. J. Kirk Sullivan
Mrs. Nancy A. Swenson
Mr. J. Warren Tompkins
The Honorable Judy Baar Topinka
Mr. Alexander F. Treadwell
Mr. Skip Vallee
Mrs. Ann Wagner
Miss Kristi A. Wallin
Representative J. C. Watts, Jr.
Representative Vin Weber
Mr. W. Edgar Welden

SENIOR STAFF

Deputy Executive Directors
Joe Ellis
Heather Larrison

*Director, Vice Presidential
Operations*
Kara Ahern

Chief Financial Officer
Eric Bing

Director, Public Liaison
Neal Burnham

Director, Events and Operations
Spencer Geissinger

Director, Official Proceedings
Bob Goodwin

General Counsel
Tom Josefiak

*Director, Ticketing
and Invitations*
Joanna McIntosh

Director, Mrs. Bush Operations
Clare Pritchett

Director, Communications
Steve Schmidt

Director, Special Services
Kate Walters

Co-Directors, Finance
Willie Gaynor
Dorinda Moss

EPICENTER MEDIA LLC

Matthew Naythons, *President*

David Hume Kennerly, *Vice President*

Dawn Sheggeby, *Editorial Director*

Tom Walker, *Creative Director*

Acey Harper, *Director of Photography*

John Silbersack, *Literary Representation*